Wake Up, Sleepwalker

ROCKY MOUNTAIN POETRY SERIES
DAVID J. ROTHMAN, EDITOR

Wake Up, Sleepwalker

Poems

Sigman Byrd

A DIVISION OF SAMIZDAT PUBLISHING GROUP

GOLDEN, COLORADO

CONUNDRUM PRESS A DIVISION OF SAMIZDAT PUBLISHING GROUP.
PO Box 1279, Golden, Colorado 80402

Wake Up, Sleepwalker

First Edition.

For information, email INFO@CONUNDRUM-PRESS.COM.

ISBN: 978-1-942280-03-3

Library of Congress Control Number: 2014951809

For my wonderful wife, Renata,
and, of course, for Chelsea and Skylar

A heartfelt thanks to Eric Burger, Ned Balbo, and
David J. Rothman for helping me see things I could not see.

Acknowledgments

Grateful acknowledgement is made to the magazines in which versions of these poems appeared:

Alaska Quarterly Review: "Apotheosis of the Great Troublemaker"; "The Great Troublemaker Makes Plans"

American Literary Review: "Listening to Shostakovich"; "The Great Troublemaker Thinks About the Soul"

Antioch Review: "Close the Book"

Ascent: "Anatomy Lab"

CEA Critic: "Opinions, Beliefs, Perspectives"; "The Kayakers"; "One Glance"

Gulf Coast: "Café de Luxe"

Marsh Hawk Review: "Diorama Against the End of History"

New Madrid: "The Golden Noumenon"; "The Great Troublemaker Waits for the Perseids"

Ocean State Review: "The Great Troublemaker"; "Now, and Now, and Now"

Ploughshares: "Diabetic"

Plume: "The Beginner"

Poetry Daily: "The Company"

Prairie Schooner: "Breathing"; "Poetry Will Never Save the World"

Southwest Review: "The Company"

Sou'wester: "The Discovery"

Tiferet: "A Letter from the World"

Table of Contents

III.

IV.

Introduction

I met Sigman Byrd several years ago when we were both teaching in the Program for Writing and Rhetoric at the University of Colorado in Boulder. He immediately conveyed a charismatic affability and we began chatting on our way to and from classes, over coffee, and as we retreated from faculty meetings. I soon learned that not only was he interested in poetry, but had published an award-winning book, *Under the Wanderer's Star*, with Marsh Hawk Press, and that we had known many of the same people at the University of Utah when we did graduate work there at different times. I then read, with delight, the early manuscripts of *Wake Up, Sleepwalker*, and when Conundrum's publisher Caleb Seeling and I hatched the plan for the Rocky Mountain Poetry Series, Sig was one of the first people I contacted.

Sig's new book might at first seem like a surprising choice to inaugurate our series. Our name identifies our books as originating in a particular corner of the planet, but Sig's poems rarely if ever refer to specific places or even regions. Towns and even streets go unnamed, as do most of the characters, with the notable exception of the Great Troublemaker, whom I take to be one of the author's *doppelgängers*.

And yet this is all as it should be, for the purpose of our series is not merely to present poetry about the Rocky Mountain west. Strong art need not make a theme out of the place where its author conceived and created it. One of the signs that a place is coming of artistic age is that it fosters any number of compelling styles. Although we will present work that does situate itself in this part of the world, our larger purpose is to publish books of significant imaginative power that address how we live and who we are.

Sig's work reminds me at times of Mark Irwin, another poet who spends much of his time in Colorado. Both poets offer us parables with a twist. Sig's poems resonate with language that directs us toward truth, and yet that truth rarely emerges as it would in simpler tales. We get the sense that there is a moral compass in these poems, but in the "pain forest" the marks remain difficult to read. There is a sense of urgency and a desire for knowledge and meaning, but the question of what we should believe and what we should do is unclear. It is not an easy place to live:

> When thinking and methods and strategies fail,
> give emptiness your letter of introduction.
>
> —"Now, and Now, and Now"

Life is a dream and yet paradise an illusion:

> *Wake up, sleepwalker.* But it's too late.
> The mind like a ship's engine rumbles to life.
> He stands on the deck and waves
> among others like him,
> passengers who think they are leaving,
> their eyes burdened and blinking
> with paradise.
>
> —"The Great Troublemaker Makes Plans"

Much of our life transpires in a "festering / / gusto of fear" ("Saturday Night Special").

Many of the poems, such as "The Company," appear to be flinty, mock odes to late consumer-capitalist alienation:

> We were alive. We had forgotten we were alive.
> We believed the company was
> the one thing we could believe in.

Yet this book goes far beyond satire and despair. There is plenty of folly on display in *Wake Up, Sleepwalker*, but Sig is not content merely to anatomize it. I keep returning to that Great Troublemaker and the way he reminds us, again and again, of the impossible necessity of completing the parables this book would weave. "The Great Troublemaker Takes in the View" —or at least he tries to—but he keeps getting comically distracted by the detritus of modern life and his own harsh self-criticism:

> . . . the sudden, sinking awareness
> that I hadn't lived a more purpose-driven life
> interrupted like an infomercial
> for the maximum ram-jam ab cruncher.

But it is exactly this distance between love, peace and harmony and the way we live now that is the didactic point. These parables feel incomplete because they do not resolve moral dilemmas, yet they do nevertheless provide guidance by provoking us to consider those dilemmas in the first place.

And in the end, in the strongest poems of the book, rightly placed as it moves towards its conclusion, Sig shows his complicated and beautiful spiritual hand. A rich belief that rises from the ashes of negation, failure and emptiness emerges without a specific theology. When "The Great Troublemaker Thinks About the Soul," he closes by saying:

> thoughts, words, the slippery rope
> of syntax that binds you to ideas—
> every day I practice letting them go.
>
> Every day I wait for you, open,
> when you come flying through the gaps.

And then, more and more, what starts to fly through those gaps, an increasingly palpable truth, is love, especially for his wife, but by extension for the entire fallen creation.

Sig is not a devout or pious poet, but he is more than merely a spiritual one. He is a religious poet in the sense that Milosz is a religious poet, or Brother Antoninus, or Hopkins, even Dante. He has been tested and his faith is both tempered and exalted by a strong draught of the void. And Sig's astute tour of that internal landscape, his telling of its subtle parables which only we can complete, is what makes this book a living part of our own landscape now, and a deeply fitting volume to inaugurate the Rocky Mountain Poetry Series.

—David J. Rothman, Editor

I.

"Can the little details of body, of breath, still be
revered and attended to? Can this, what's sunk into
our bones, be the lattice on which awareness grows?"
—Ryushin Paul Haller

The Beginner

Doesn't have a clue, sips whiskey in a train
station on the other side of thought, imagining

the space between the days, the votive cells
and atoms of each moment rising. Says *yes*

to everything that happens, fails egregiously
and says *yes* again. Believes in no birth, no death,

in the engine full of apples fermenting
among garlands of sunshine and farewell kisses,

believes the engine as greater vehicle of transcendence
has been corrupted. *What is it?* he asks.

But he forgets how answers are stitched together.
Feels the self-same swing of speech and silence

and fashions his own answer, the rookie inside
each of us, the newcomer squeezing a lemon wedge

into a glass of autumnal sighs. Regrets and
wrong turns, the body exposed to the golden wind.

How can this human life be anything other than
astonishing? The *tick-tick-tick* of pleasure's ignition

quietly catching—after all these years, the one who
has just arrived knows exactly what to do.

Breathing

It happens without my paying much attention:
the regular rise and fall of the chest,
air rushing through the moist wind tunnels
of the throat and nose, that sweet God muscle,
life's soft engine, the diaphragm,
contracting and relaxing whenever I climb
the stairs or need a little comfort
after a gloomy day.

Maybe in another time and place
beyond the melancholy shores of goodbye,
I could honor this forgotten kindness.
I could close my laptop and listen
to the slip-and-lock rhythm,
those two blessed, sing-song notes sung
ten or fifteen times a minute every day.

Maybe I just lifted a heavy bag of cement
or the shaven tires on my car
lost their traction in a snowstorm,
and then suddenly, miraculously,
they found it again.

He's catching his breath,
someone would say if they saw me
sobbing on the side of the road.
And then, the slow, deep intake awakens me.
The letting go and pushing out marry me
to the body. No thoughts,
just the clear, affirming gap
between breaths. For one or two seconds,
the still point
when the world and I are one.

A Letter from the World

Not that you didn't recognize the dragonfly
dallying on the zipper of your backpack
         or register the bulbous
black, compound eyes
and segmented abdomen as they dipped
and bobbed over the rapids.

You were expert at observing appearances,
the iridescent blue-green wings
fluttering, cantilevered above
         the inky flow, ready to hover
or bolt in ten directions
and then the water at your feet
sheering into the tall creek grasses.

But what you saw was what you added:
plunge and purpose, color flash and story,
         the old narrative tick triggering
into motion the unending deluge
                  of desire.

Hear me out. You were drained
by looking, swiftly circulating
through dust off cliff face and trailhead,
         busy.
Maybe you never truly learned to sit
for one moment by the creek's phototropic glimmer,
         or hear the sizzling grains
of sunlight crawl through the aspens.

Maybe you are the one I dreamed
would come some day,

the one smitten with the apocrypha
of measurable things,
          the one almost ready
                    for emptiness.

Zen Garden

One whimsical shift of perception
and the boulder arranged in the raked gravel
inflates into a windswept,
sea-thrashed island where I imagine
a sun-tanned Robinson Crusoe version of myself
roasting clams over a roaring campfire.

I wake up each morning, hike the rock's cut crack.
Its trickle of moisture,
from this oddball angle,
looks like a misty, hibiscus-dappled stream
where I pause on my way,
sipping water from a coconut cup.

Next, the clean, flowing lines of gravel.
In the blink of an eye, they transform
into a booming surf at high tide
beyond which no ship's rigging, no painted hull
or Friday has passed in years.

Move back out again, and in the fathomless
hush between waves,
the whole ocean starts to feel
miniature. A wisp of string blows in,
but from where I'm sitting on my lotus blossom bench,
it could be a thick coil of sailor's rope,
a castaway's treasure
washed up on the hot sand.

Perfect for hitching my hammock
between two towering palms,
or, depending on the vicissitudes of the season,
lashing my homemade
lizard-skin tent in a gale.

The Great Troublemaker

I don't remember when or how he arrived.
All I know is he must have tucked
himself in at the beginning.

The blanket was warm, the milk free.
The ones called parents ogled me
and cooed. They repeated

the sibilant sound of a name,
and into that almost audible Eden
an awareness fell, the molten slag

and guttural snap of *I*, the unappeasable
story, the words in the mouth
of the one who would be me:

I want kangaroo juice, he spluttered.
Put the red elephant here, he demanded.
Then the cold commencing

from which no one escapes. Cuddly,
red Bandoola, the fiction of a unified
world had its stuffing torn out.

The blanket coarse to the touch,
the fort of cushions he huddled in
massive but fragile, I don't remember

when or how his tantrum became
my tantrum, the great troublemaker's
theatrical cargo of suffering.

Mine, all mine, I lugged it with me
like a song, a mewling lullaby
I could never stop singing.

Now, and Now, and Now

No need to ask, no stopping either, no path.
Call off the search teams.
That river running with snowmelt is your home.
That foaming, seaweed-tangled cove is
your body—yes, yours,
the rotating cliffs, the distracted winds and valleys.
Like one who has forgotten,
you peek into the smoky crevices of the heart.
You roll down the window as you pass,
and all you see are the cracked,
tarnished mirrors of yesterday and tomorrow,
dead letter tunnels, extinct, fossilized regions.

Let this be the final warning: you drive.
The frosty wheel of heaven turns.
The sun's indefatigable warmth travels 93 million miles
to smooch your face. Let bygones be bygones.
Your life remains intact like a blinking streetlight
at three A.M. And now that you have buried yourself,
or rather now that you have set up shop
in the Ritalined, regolithic vapors of thought,
go ahead and slide into the drive-thru carwash
with your big, new minivan.
Let it float out the other side, sparkling,
paramour of change embarking on a fresh excursion
past the Starbucks and KFC,
past the wholesale megastore bursting
with posh microclimates of tennis racquets and treadmills.
Let life sink in tenaciously like a three-car garage
on the outer banks of a loneliness you call your own.
Now, and now, and now, it says,
I am the one who will find you.

When thinking and methods and strategies fail,
give emptiness your letter of introduction.
Mention the parking lots pocked with muddy potholes,
the high-occupancy concrete of express lanes
willing to jimmy you anywhere.
Then highlight the abundance of arpeggios,
juke-joint blues and tender, oceanic sonatas plucked
from cassette tapes jammed in the dashboard,
the countless Iliads and Odysseys spring composes
in green shoots and junkets of rain.
Discuss the intimate grassy knolls
and desolate football stadiums beside every
plow-county blacktop where even now
someone turns the pages,
listens to the sunshine, sings the questions.

Emptiness, that palpitating birthplace of form;
emptiness, the space where mountains walk
and a stone woman gives birth
to a child. You and everyone
in the lanes around you empty, like you,
in whom glances and billboards, destinies and voices
pass unscathed, without speeding, gifted,
like a zephyr of red, excitable days.
Swear to me you've had enough
of the riffraff in your moo-moo.
Swear to me now, before the next exit,
you've had enough of illusions.

The Last Door

If a time before doors ever existed,
I couldn't say: a door here to mark
my passage through, a door there to frame
my fetching face time and get-togethers consummated,
and then doors of people congregating
on the tarmac, pecking at tiny glass screens,
either before or after
in the law-abiding field of vision.

And thinking this way, I began to understand
how a landscape divides
into inside or outside, me versus them.
January, the blizzard flung the snowy, wet towel of its rage,
but I pictured somewhere a well-lit door
with metal kick plates opening and closing.

My name was called.
I stood up and took my place in line.
A door, resplendent with knob and lock,
knocker and nameplate, hung on its hinges
like the painting of a door. *A super door*, I thought,
not a door of the mind, not a monstrous replica.

I hoped it carried in its molecules
a moxied mojo I could have confidence in.
I hoped behind it life was about to begin
its hair-brained blitzkrieg.
In a minute I'll be golden, I said,
the crack of bone on wood like the sleepless door
of an apostle's longing.
Thinking and waiting and believing
like a stone rolled back
only to reveal a door woven out of air,

the quickening door of care,
personal, on which I couldn't stop knocking,
from which I never dared to wake up.

Only Child, Two A.M.

Alone in her thoughts on a worried side of town,
she strolled past the My Office Club
and the yoga center,
peered in the windows at the tropical fish store
and a shop brimming with used
barber chairs and dusty hairdryers
big as thrones.

Then, out of the corner of her right eye,
as if down a darkened tunnel
in an ancient telescope,
she caught a glimpse of her reflection.
Her again: the demure,
oddly thin chin; the golden tresses
out of some boozy, whoring fairytale.

Such vivid dreams! In the morning
she always remembered them:
the smell of singed hair; scissors
grazing her rosy scalp. Dreams of grieving
without end, she thought,
like beauty's stepsisters, the really good ones
she knew she could count on.

The Great Troublemaker Makes Plans

Don't wake him, the old wisdom says.
But let him traipse the planks
     of this dreaming world
as if he were sleepwalking onboard
a ghost ship about to set sail for a remote
and tropical island getaway.

It's the story of his life and won't let go.
His departure is delayed—again.
He complains with words he finds on his lips,
     sea-wracked, foam-heavy words
he is actually speaking.

Even now, he believes,
people like him dressed in festively colored,
micro-fiber sunwear are sipping drinks
     with exotic names somewhere
and listening to the pleasing cadences
of pulsing steel drums. Even now the earth
     is turning and tomorrow,
somewhere, is rising.

Wake up, sleepwalker. But it's too late.
The mind like a ship's engine rumbles to life.
He stands on the deck and waves
     among others like him,
passengers who think they are leaving,
their eyes burdened and blinking
     with paradise.

Diorama Against the End of History

On certain hot summer nights,
he could hear in the simmering
nets of leaves on maple trees
Immanuel Kant wind his pocket watch
or, if he listened carefully,

Gustave Mahler tap his cane,
wondering if this conspicuous season
was a major or minor outing.
Other nights the wind got personal.
Branches snapped, gusts of black

rain pounded like a hurt so old
and hallowed he couldn't let go.
And what was it? The scissor-cut
of lightning, a salvo of thunder
terrifying like adult voices

sparring in the next room?
He tried to forget the details,
every nicety and modulation of tone,
as if by an act of immaculate denial
he could comfort the little boy

soaked and running for cover,
even at this late hour the winged
seeds and shattered twigs
of the past still flying through
the haunted forest of his thoughts.

II.

"He wore a hat and he had a job and he brought home the bacon."

—Devo

The Great Troublemaker Waits for the Perseids

Tonight I am watching a TV show about meteors,
a full hour of atmospheric voiceovers
and high-def motion graphics depicting collisions
of frozen rock and metal, space debris
tumbling in slow motion
as it enters Earth's atmosphere and catches flame
like a Chevy Camaro riding the shockwave
of another beautifully choreographed explosion
on a rerun of "Starsky and Hutch."
But then a pledge break interrupts.
A chatty senior citizen with a white pompadour
urges me to join the community
of civic-minded viewers giving fifty,
seventy-five, a hundred dollars a month.

I smile—it's that time of year again
when what matters most is the size of my wallet.
Meanwhile, this talking head on TV, this pitch man
for all things chock full and charitable,
rolls up his sleeves so I can admire the tanned,
youthful luster of his arms. He reminds me
I'm a riot of dream babble, a target demographic
of coded longing conjured by a focus group,
a survey of satisfied customers.

So I turn off the TV and open the sliding glass door.
I step outside and breathe.
If any super-chunk, solar system-hopping boulders
are streaking obliviously through the sky
tonight, I hope I will see them.
But the only things moving are the shadowy
SUVs floating past the dim,
iodine-orange glow of the street light,

the pale, snappy flashes escaping the windows
across the street where the flat-screen,
surround-sound plasma TVs cast
their medicinal spell on my neighbors.

We are stardust, Joni Mitchell once sang,
billion-year-old carbon, we are golden.
I am trying to swim to the shoreline
without getting sucked under. It's like the movie
where the main character, this aw-shucks
everyman accountant, discovers his wife wants
a divorce, and as he reads her seething
text message, he reaches out to touch the moon.
But it glows like a phosphorescent,
photoshopped ad on steroids,
the clear night sky drifts in like a form
of product placement, and the exhausted words
streaming out of the actor's mouth push something
that sounds like a great, gassy atmosphere
of superheated sand and rock, a meteor shower
(a real one, dear God)
careening irreversibly toward the heartland,
the hypnotherapeutic strip malls and suburbs
flashing on the screen before disappearing
into thin air above us.

The Company

We believed in the company as permanent gravity,
as sacrament, and got the job done.
We were given the memo about getting it done.
But then the company changed hands.
Another, more profitable company
hoisted up a sign and told us
the product line "needed adjusting."
We were told.
And the company, like a beneficent scrim
of blackened sky, pure space—
we looked up into it after a hard day,
everything in it glowing and turning,
a spray of light patterned into
an elastic, expansive aura we began
to envision as living.

We listened to the forklifts whir
through the company, delivering things,
sending things away.
It sounded like a cube of restless ocean
under a coil of glistening weather.
It breathed like who we were
when we donned our protective suits
and flashed our data cards. *Good morning*, we said
and imagined the company's flinty, flexible shell
resembled something deep inside us.
We believed in our work
as sympathetic blueprint, as touchable.
We were alive. We had forgotten we were alive.
We believed the company was
the one thing we could believe in.

The New Money

What signals its relevance is the founding father's
ghostly, floating, off-center head propped
into a neck tourniquet and cape so that he resembles
a disembodied vampire. The watermark positioned to
the right of the portrait and the digital security thread
that glows red when exposed to ultraviolet light
complicate the presentation and will frustrate viewers
who see it with dubious motives, bundled into
stacks, say, and counted into suitcases.

But the work also functions as commentary
on the perpetual allure of conspiracy theories.
Critics point to cryptic Latin phrases,
pyramids and all-seeing eyes, peculiar likenesses
of the flaming World Trade Center
embedded in the shifting color-field. Proof, they say,
of a sinister plot. But this misses the real point:
its addictive allure, its fluid, fungible ability
to manufacture whole categories of longing.

Picked out of purses, positioned on little plastic trays
slipped into envelopes, buried in attic walls,
fought over and aspired to, the work now trends
to a previously unheard-of level of popularity,
a major, new addition to the Found Art movement.
This bill, for example, a twenty, discovered
just this morning at the corner of Broadway and Pearl,
a pure readymade carefully rendered,
dropped on the curb near a parking meter,
crumpled like a tossed-out candy wrapper.
When no one was looking,
I reached down and grabbed it.

Later I will move among the aisles of glossy,
shrink-wrapped merchandise. I will feel the imperturbable
force and flow of how a wallet opens as I look
into the eyes of customer service champion
Tim or Ahmad, the high school kid with the gold-stud earring
awaiting payment, and I will hand it to him.
We will smile our contractual smiles.
He will take my cash, our ritual gestures of power
and submission to power not exactly
an American original but a classic display
of penetrating performance art.

Lock and Load

His mouth moves
with the logic of ash and cinders.
Persistent, put upon,
for the cameras, he warns
in a starry nebula of conjecture
something sinister has entered the valley.

We watch him believe what he is saying.
We watch him believe soon the wind,
soon the holy city will be stained
with pestilent shadows, once and for all
the gold standard will return.

And it sounds real this time.
It sounds like the premonition
of a prosperous and loving astronaut,
so we listen. We tune in each morning.
We think of him when we go to sleep at night.

We imagine him chanting in the desert
preparing his trailer among the stars.
Soon ground will be broken, he says.
Soon fiber optic cables will pierce
the magnanimous mantle of the earth.
Soon bankers and yes men
will be handing over our names.
Are we ready?

We watch him brush a tear
from his eye. He says, even as we speak.
He says, beware the hackers,
the whacked cabal meeting in Washington,
and he assures us he is on our side.

He says, the four horseman come,
the seven golden vials
bubbling with the wrath of God.
He says, prepare yourself.
He says he wants to know,
are we ready?

Saturday Night Special

I chanced on it one Sunday morning
snug in the glittering outside my house.

Shy pud of the barrel, Lilliputian grip perfect
for a child's hand or an heiress's purse.

When I imagined it tossed from the car window,
a bullet still breathing in the chamber,

or spiraling fleshward, unincarnate,
at two-hundred feet per second, there was

nothing that hadn't already smeared me
in its awful trajectory and tawdry aftermath.

Oh, don't ask if or why I carried it inside,
joy-swilling, hate-monger widow maker.

Like someone surrounded, a crime
on his hands, at home in the festering

gusto of fear, I aimed it at the window.
It shamed me. It blamed me, anyone but me.

How easily my finger perched on
the slippery pull-weight of the trigger.

Fly away, I said. But it wasn't a bird,
and out there, no sliver of peaceable sky.

The Great Troublemaker Takes in the View

I was sitting under a soaring cliff face and listening
to the icy rush of water, like a Buddhist monk
      in an ancient forest monastery,
letting heaven and earth take their turns,
when a feeling coursed through my body
as if this total stranger vegging on my sofa
      was channel surfing,
and the sudden, sinking awareness
that I hadn't lived a more purpose-driven life
      interrupted like an infomercial
            for the maximum ram-jam ab cruncher.

I dipped my hand in the water and drew an arrow
in the thick, muddy silt. I imagined
a tingling filament of calm
      threading into my arms. But my thoughts
      like an old LP record kept skipping
to a top-forty song about a nagging lack
and then onto another song about the self-cleaning,
      aerodynamically designed city of tomorrow
where I hoped to move one day.

I got back in the car and drove home.
I cracked open the latest Deepak Chopra.
      With splendid powers of concentration,
I put on my yoga pants and practiced Downward Dog
and Bird of Paradise on the deck
in the middle of the afternoon.
      And just when I thought it was safe,
      I heard a tinkling bell as on the edge of the yard,
as if some lovable, loyal mutt had bounded over the fence
with his toy, panting, tossing it in the air,
racing over so we could play. Oh, mind,

incorrigible creature of habit,
your trigger-happy synapses, your voluptuous neural pathways
blipped with another distraction:
the kid across the street bouncing
a blue basketball, his oversized Lebron James jersey,
which reminded me
of the two-year, $42 million deal
the basketball superstar signed to play in Cleveland.

Interrogation

That I had something to say was a virtue.
They loved the tank, they said, facing down violent protesters.
They loved the ladders and inflatable slides offering
a way out of the burning fuselage.
Would I care to comment?
I said there was a pain forest
in which many gray, sticky trees had been constructed,
in which renters and homeowners
alike waited it out.

This only piqued their curiosity. They suggested
I mention my position vis-à-vis
the counter-insurgency, the strafing of the gene pool,
progress. They said I should think about
the overall quality of my portfolio.
They said I should say something.

But the scenarios flashed their high-beams.
Stillness laminated the pontoon bridge.
I sensed my heart no longer belonged to the avenue of forms.
They sensed my lack of a vetted media outlet,
so they locked the doors, pulled out
their hot tongs and clipboards.
I prepared myself for the "consequences."
They drove the issue through a heavy crosswind.
I ate a sack lunch of peaches and sacks.
What was form, I told them, if not an appetizer
of flambéed isotopes on the à la carte menu of vacancy?
Their codes were sagging. They wanted
resources: a chancellery perhaps;
a sweet and sour theory of articulated gestures,
something they could hang their hats on.

I thanked them. I got out of there as quickly as I could.
The provincial towns reported gunfire.
The transformers and broadcast towers were down.
A full moon rose over headquarters
in another rotating, consumable display.
But I was tired of laying the groundwork.
I had something to say so I ran.
My home the silence called, my home the emptiness,
my home the three doors beyond saying.

The Golden Noumenon

Don't get me wrong, I'm not unhappy with our progress:
the enormous effort expended to create sophisticated
digital phone networks or the season's new, more colorful lawn furniture.
Somewhere at this very moment
      all over the world
strategically organized and astoundingly profitable corporations
      are getting the job done.
Polycrystalline diamond drill bits bore into the earth.
Mountains of superheated cement are pumped through hoses.
      Faces monitor shifting, colossal numbers
on computer screens—all for the sake of our glistening,
stain-resistant, non-negotiable
      quality of life.

But let me be clear. Those faces—
with eyes blinking in lovely, indecipherable patterns,
      with thoughts and feelings,
predilections rotating in and out of moist lips and rows of teeth,
      with identities and career tracks
      spoken and unspoken—
they're human faces. I've seen them. Inside each one
the golden noumenon, an unseen, unheard
awareness cries out, *Here I am.*

Can you hear it? It's tearing into the counterfeit quietude
manufactured daily for us
      micron by unholy micron.
It's there in the whispering spruce forest,
in the clanging shipping container clogged with trees
and lumber cut screaming from the logs,
      that voice, that open, intimate voice
that wants to be embodied, called out from,
and fit into like a cashmere sweater.

It's there, too, in the exchange
of credit card numbers, in the manager's two-for-one sale
on nails and drywall, glue guns and plywood,
in the doll houses and coffins
constructed from plywood, in the dust that coats
the TV consoles when no one is looking,
when the children are long gone,
in the peer-reviewed papers where the words are written
that no one will remember.

I'm touching it. I'm holding it in my hand like a small,
nameless visitor, a bird from a distant,
unauthorized forest no one's ever walked in. *Here I am*:
the golden noumenon, the voice, the one thing
we are incontrovertibly gifted with,
the flare that wasn't expected,
a late awareness before the information arrives,
before the news of money and the collecting of frou-frou,
before desire and its habits of exhaustion.
On the far side of language, in unmitigated clarity,
the call packets diverted, the websites shut down,
can you hear it? It waits for us.
It has no mobile phone number. It cannot be taken away.

Crossing Over

O dharma electricity, flowing wheatfield,
indestructible wedding guest, I lay the burnt
offerings of my ambition outside your tent.
Its dust will pollinate the windshields of cars everywhere.
I relinquish my taxidermy, my tuneful fiddle faddle.
When the dance floor was littered with confetti,
you turned up the lights on all mental projections.
They glistened with attitude. I sprayed them
with epoxy resin that would last a thousand years.
Then the prayer flags were planted.
The new uber-faces were the same as the old uber-faces.
I learned from them. Even now I lick your great
plebeian ocean liner when it churns into the harbor.
I search for the slow lightning, the magnetic
esprit de corps. Open, crackling, pellucid, like you
I drive without mirrors and brake lights,
without tires, without turning the radio on.
I pack a toothbrush and a flare gun. I listen
to the cosmos pinging like an irascible submarine.
When I die my bloodline will vanish, my starcharts
crumble. I will walk in the boundlessness
with a higher deductible yet no benefits package.
I will eat pomegranates in the gloaming.
As you have shown me, there will be no debriefing.
I will leave no voice behind to follow.

Café de Luxe

What people say adds up to something. I still believe
that or want to anyway.
I can mention ghosts and God and still sound
reasonable. I can glance under the hood
at the greasy, spinning belts.

The problem is no one pays attention anymore,
or maybe they do as in the peculiar way
a bar of soap listens to the rain
outside. You there, for example,

are you listening? I picture the old footage
of you reclining in those Brunswick bowling-alley chairs.
Patiently, you wait for the chorus to return:
a catchy tune you can snap your finger to;
pizzicatos by the dusky sea.

I try to win you over, but the two women
in the next booth are kissing. A spoon clicks
against a glass of iced tea.
I'm sure you've read about it on the Internet,
the little Bic butane flame of distraction
and desire between two people or one person and an idea,
the shimmy of skirt and pant legs
or skirt and skirt,
wouldn't mind if I did,
around a little hat with many sides, multiple
visions of itself ultimately believable but hard
to imagine like Charles's ugly childhood
helmet in *Madame Bovary*.

Are you still there? Perhaps you should see me
at your earliest convenience, as I have
some potentially life-changing news to tell you.

And don't forget, I am with you
in the peculiar way
a bar of soap whispers back to the rain outside.
I am with you in the dance of forms
so prominent and palpable one moment
and then gone the next.

Who We Were

In the future, forensic scientists will train
a laser beam on a bone chip or hair particle,
on the tell-tale chemical bonds
hidden in a spectral smear of molecules
and understand everything about how we lived.
From the composite resin of a tooth filling,
a portrait of our passion for curly fries and mojitos.
From a cracked circuit board,
our spending habits and hobbies, our obsession
with drug-addled Hollywood movie stars,
and our complete and utter disregard for poetry.

An open-and-shut case, they will say
of our illustrious days carousing on Earth.
Then in their omnipotent tweezers, they will hold up
a charred, crumbling slip of paper
on which our final testament is written.
Get a load of this, they will say.
And in the standardized, quick-coat, four-color
pixeling of ink, they will ascertain the hired script
of a copywriter sitting at a borrowed desk.
Someone like you or me with responsibilities,
bills to pay, twin daughters who wanted
the same shiny, purple bicycle with tassels,
someone who once in a blue moon
would look out the window at night and imagine. . . .

Imagine what? they will ask.
But here is where the trail of sequenced photons,
the strung particles and nano signatures
of evidence they will examine under their well-lubricated
microscopes turns cold. As if behind their backs
when no one was looking

dark matter of an untouchable noumenon,
the ineffable breach in a quantum personal seam
was speeding through the galaxies, pictures of who we were,
smiling and waving, when we of that time
are nowhere else to be found.

Nightshade

So these are the much-anticipated
dark nights of the soul
philosophers and saints
talk about.

Long, dark nights
like the ones on TV:
gout-ridden investment bankers
counting their stacks;

guilty priests confessing
to you know who.
The kind of nights best spent
tending one's innermost hunches.

But then the sneaking suspicion
nothing inside or innermost
was left. In its place,
a screaming newspaper headline

on a touch screen,
a cricket chirping to a beer bottle
on a patio draped
with strange, overgrown plants,

the succulent red teardrops of berries
beneath a moon
the color of approaching battles
in the late August sky.

III.

"What, then, does one know of You? Only everything.
For one no longer knows particulars."
—Martin Buber

The Great Troublemaker Thinks About the Soul

I wait for you, monkeyshine,
white-throated thrummer of silence,

but every day asks me to accept the premise
you do not exist, or if you do,

the kindled message you carry is
a fable of wishful thinking.

Even this longing for you, the story goes,
broods and burns of its own volition.

Well, that may be. But if long ago
someone wearing a bearskin hide felt you,

quirky and unnamable, move inside him
and drew on the cave wall

a fleet-footed, magical beast,
he must've conjured also the narrow

mountain pass that allowed your escape.
Thoughts, words, the slippery rope

of syntax that binds you to ideas—
every day I practice letting them go.

Every day I wait for you, open,
when you come flying through the gaps.

Diabetic

To imagine the sweetness pushing through my veins
like grains of glass scarring a beach
when the tide sweeps in.
To prick my finger and squeeze
a drop of blood, angel rich, earth heavy,
onto a test strip.

To wait for the meter as it counts,
and stare past the little black numbers
all the way back to the inflamed nerves, the capillaries.
To say I am tied to the body
like a backcountry skier awash in
a wave of crimson snow.

And the lows,
those moments when I shuffle off the cliff.
To forget who I am, cold-coated in sweat,
slurring into unconsciousness.
To feel the mind reduced to a motor
blasted into parts.

To hear my wife pleading with me,
Come on, wake up, she says.
To say the pangs and shocks of flesh
are my inheritance,
and life loaded,
if I am to believe in it, begins in the blood,

that I may listen to it chatter,
that I may learn its reckless language
coming and going,
primitive hearsay
whenever I spoon the honey,
whenever I stuff the bread in my mouth.

The Word

When you brush your silky, black hair
and show me the portable savanna of your waist,
I hear it flutter inside you.
Like a laundromat whispering in winter
or a tree limb falling on Madison Avenue,
only softer, it wants to articulate something.
But what exactly?
You bend down to check your voicemail.
You raise your arms over your head
in the manner of Rutherford B. Hayes.

Meanwhile, solar winds caress the unknown
sentence in which the word appears
like a newly discovered planet.
And I, who have always believed too much
in naming, let the mystery in:
the compact curve of your hips plumping
the blue nightie; the red spiral notebook
where you write your morning pages,
sipping a cup of African rooibos tea.

Surely, such a vision suggests this life
is composed of discreet, fetching and lovable
packages of meaning. Show it to me, hon,
the healing adjective, the scorched gerund.

Point me to the path
where eventually I may stumble
across the hurt you carry like a secret amulet.
Let me be the one who is listening
when the word billows over the rustic peaks
and electrifies the skidding,
saturated sky of your thoughts.

Like

The honking of geese in fog is like
a mischievous car horn
I heard once on the crowded *zocalo*
in Oaxaca. And both are like
the spangled ballroom of the mind,

a Saturday night full of dancers
strutting through the world
of appearances, negotiating a line through,
yoking themselves
to another preposterous rhythm.

But when I see you mashing overripe bananas
into a bowl of flour, hon,
you are nothing like the mind.
Still, all I have are the glib sound bites of simile,
metaphor's fickle inexactitude.

You chop the walnuts, and I gaze
into the scribbled orchids of your eyes.
You gaze back as if we are already
there together, passports stamped
in that rarely visited, impractical country

where a sleeping volcano
nestles up to a deep green lake,
where we lie in each other's arms
and the steady afternoon rain
falling on a tin roof falls exactly like rain.

Poetry Will Never Save the World

You sit down to read it
and the lines maintain a strict, irreversible
silence like one of those submarines
that periodically sinks to the bottom of the ocean
and begins filling up with cold, dark water.
You wait for a radio signal then,
a tapping on the hull—anything
to prove those intrepid, young men
are hanging on.

But poetry never surfaces.
Its hulk becomes a living reef
that teems with seaweed and sponges,
colorful fish with evocative names,
darting in and out of unseen,
unverified grammatical crevices.
You open a book, and if you're lucky on occasion,
you find yourself sitting against a tree
in the middle of an ancient forest,
all around you masters of the climate:
wet stones, decaying logs, roots bearded
with lichens, a canopy of green shadows.

And peeking out of the leaves, so you might
easily miss them, tiny yellow and purple flowers
drip with rainwater. They are the words
of the poem you are reading,
a poem whose only purpose,
a spot out of time, is pleasure:

I am the people's point of view, a cow,
the tropical wind, I sleep under the surface.
I am the aristocratic carnivore, I eat form.
I drum on cooks' white caps, I drum on their aprons . . .

The words have nothing to say
or add to you. But you listen to them.
They take you where you need to go.

Love Triangle

I want to write a poem for you, but I'm afraid
      it will be less than perfect,

won't last or even reject me after all I've done for it.
      So I take out the trash.

I tell myself I will scratch out a few seductive syllables
      after I spiff up the kitchen.

Next morning the page gazes up at me like a long
      forgotten lover draping herself

across my desk. And the words, when I read them,
      vibrate suggestively on my tongue.

They mention what I want to do with you when
      you wear those old camo pants,

or when the thin, black spaghetti straps on your dress
      topple deliciously off your shoulders

at Home Depot. *Finish me*, the poem says.
      But it bristles when I mouth

the word *you*. It swoons over you, your long
      black hair, your easy laugh.

And now I think the poem wants to forget me.
      Or maybe it just wants to keep me

around long enough, hostage to its starlit hegemony,
      till I mention your job

at the windchime factory, your unforeseen generosity
      the time after a rough day

you brought in two steaming bowls of homemade
        miso soup. But when it talks

like this, smitten with you, relentlessly revised,
        no longer listening, I know it's over

between the poem and me. *You are all I ever wanted,*
        I say. But it's too late. The poem

has packed its bags, ready for your eager hands
        opening the letter, the ecstasy

of your questioning gaze, all things I adore,
        waiting for me at your house.

Like Silt Unlocked in the Astral Flow

My antsy, eight-months-pregnant wife
perches on the living room sofa texting a message,
   and for this brief seed-drop in time,
it's clear: in a far-flung flexing of stars,
in a molten, subatomic tumbling
   of particles and waves a billion years ago
a red gas giant went supernova
whose sudden incandescence set off
a pyroclastic chain of events that pushes onward
to this day, flowing and eating, raining down
on galaxies and simmering in her smile.

Baby, I got booze and cigarettes, I tell her,
how 'bout we get a little frisky in the next room?
   Her firm, compact hand
around my neck, she reels me in for a kiss.
Maybe the reason for such unpremeditated bliss
is that ten minutes earlier I forgot
lifting weights at the gym.

   Fifty years before that,
my wife's mother, like a planet with its swollen axis
tilted toward the sun, kissed Japan goodbye
so she could marry a man in America,
a blossoming only possible because
   twenty years earlier
Chiang Kai-shek's threadbare, scurvy-bitten army
camped in the homes of the Taiwanese,
forcing them to flee, a few of them
like my wife's grandfather, all the way to Tokyo.

And whatever to whomever happened before that
—who can say? We live in the star flash

between conceivable worlds,
moment by moment comprised of a million
fleeting, accumulated decisions,
a woven brocade of cause and effect,
chance and intention, an unheard stream rushing
    through us at breakneck speed.

How blessed that my wife and I found each other,
rootless travelers who made it this far.
Lovesick, caught off guard,
    lives like silt unlocked in the astral flow—
such history behind her smart-alecky grin
when she says, *you bastard,*
look at what you've done to me.
Now go get me some Cool Ranch Doritos and ice water.

Witness

I, transmitter, collector of shadows,
eater of images, flip the page of the magazine.
I arrange and rearrange
⠀⠀⠀⠀⠀the brutal tumble of light
as if I could still hold on.

In one photo, a boy doused in gasoline,
enfolded in flames. His right arm
punches through a swarming fireball
⠀⠀⠀⠀⠀as if to warn the viewer.
On the facing page, beneath a 36-point,
sans serif Mission Gothic headline,
⠀⠀⠀⠀⠀the grassy hedge where the boy, lit,
had screamed, now a coffee cart,
men in straw fedoras,
bougainvilleas in bloom again.

I flip the page. The story begins.
One day soon, it says, no one alive will remember.
⠀⠀⠀⠀⠀It says the bakery opens for business,
men play dominoes where just last week
a protestor, pulled-in, closed the eyelids
⠀⠀⠀⠀⠀of a pregnant woman
shot in the neck during a demonstration.

Time the throttle point and exit wound.
⠀⠀⠀⠀⠀Time the incurable kiss.
I flip the page, and the young woman
in green hijab blinks. She still stares
⠀⠀⠀⠀⠀at the camera beside
an ad for a tough-haul, all-terrain pickup.

For now, blood pouring from her nose,
there's hope. For now, I help keep her alive.

The shutter snaps.
The street lingers with particular details,
the nuanced chiaroscuro of a specific time of day,
            people and objects
where as long as I keep looking,   •
I'm certain a calamitous meaning
            will compose itself.

The Discovery

I must be asleep,
and this life—the only one
I know—like an ant
trapped in amber
hangs from the ear of
an unknown god.

Somewhere
you, too, are sleeping.
The moon drags its briny
sleeve across the plains.
Far away, I could say, far away.

Who am I then
when the clouds turn oily and black?
Who are you when charred
fingers of paper
rain from the sky?

On one of them
your name is written.
Personal, it falls into my hands.
For one moment,
the myth of the personal:

I had no idea
it would take me this long
to find you.

Apotheosis of the Great Troublemaker

So the years began to pass like a giant sequoia
on the slow road to becoming a hand-carved footstool.

Everywhere he turned there he was: the street
of sleepwalkers on their secret pilgrimage,

that long, anonymous street of original sorrow.
As if God were everywhere, said an old man dancing

across a greasy cardboard stage, hobbled and weaving
in the grip of some private tarantella.

As if God were everywhere, and the great troublemaker,
who knew nothing about the intimate

choreography of flesh, as if for the first time,
felt his arms begin to sway and his feet begin to tap.

IV.

"When you see plum blossoms or hear the sound of a
small stone hitting bamboo,
that is a letter from the world of emptiness."
—Shunryu Suzuki

May It Be So

What I sought to attain was already here.
      My heart oriented between
the cloudless sky and the clear moon,

between the shadows of the tree
                       and the tree itself
      agitated in the token yard.

Yet I settled on the cushion. As if to say
      I am not dreaming. As if
the moonlight drilled down
          in plentiful, affiliated gusts.

I planted my knees
      and straightened my spine.
         Right hand holding left hand,

thumb tips touching in a mudra
      of nothing left to do.

If you want to climb a mountain,
      Eihei Dogen said, *start at the top.*
So I took in a breath and slowly

             let it out.

Let it crumble. A few tittering thoughts
      lingered.
But they didn't stay for long.
         What I sought to attain
was already here.

And as a dragon gains the water,
        as a tiger enters the whispering
mountains, I gazed through

the white wall in front of me
            and did not move.

Opinions, Beliefs, and Perspectives

The creek doesn't have them.
Neither do the ponderosa pines along the steep,
knotted banks. And the rocks lodged in
      the creek don't know
they rest for now surrounded by icy water.
Nor do they feel the water, chilled,
unpotable or pure, gurgling along
their slick, mineral-veined sides.

The water, meanwhile, snowmelt from somewhere
deep in the interior, doesn't call itself
      water, is unaware of being
called, of flowing around the scarred side
of the mountain, flowing into a hiker's cup,
      falling and flowing
into the blue, cloudless sky.

As for me, called to the creek,
for a few minutes, I let the world
trundle on without commenting,
no separate viewpoints.
      Everywhere I look
I see myself walking. I am not the water
but it clearly is me, a flowing gate
without qualities or need for proof,
a creek made of diamonds
uncalled—oh, nameless traveler—
      falling and flowing, broken open
by ten thousand blades of sunlight.

One Glance

The walking stick leaned
against a boulder at the creek's edge.
Let the record show for three days
        the bolt of wood
with its crooked notch and fraying
décolletage was all that remained
of the hiker and his song.

On the fourth day, an office worker
from the nearby business park
        noticed a cut-rate javelin,
a gnarled nub for old men, one glance,
and tossed it into the water.

Or maybe enchanted with the creek
        inside him, lunching
by the chilled auroras of water,
bagged and burned out, he never
saw the stick or imagined

the splinters and fibers, slim, snapped-off
furniture of idealists, a child's telescope,
the way you could point it
and peer into the prodigal kingdoms of air.
        One glance and he gazed
right through it, never
to ponder the possibility

of his own aching feet, the deathless
generosity of common things,
never to ask, wandering,
of no fixed address: what is a day
        without sticks?

The Kayakers

Some of them scrape against the boulders;
others get tangled in the weeds and detritus
along the slick, late-spring banks.
           Still others, a few perhaps,
understand how to read the current,
gauge depth and speed,
and shoot through the rapids.

For them, no distraction, no time for fear.
They paddle their sleek fiberglass boats
through the shining water.
They negotiate the froth and boil
           with skill, illumination
as if well-versed in the fable of down creek,
not tempted by the titivating images of arrival.

And then one boatman by himself, always one
like a monk in a monastery
           of shimmering
cottonwood trees and sky, sunlight smashing
through the canyon around him—

he bows and dips his hand in the creek
before launching. The boat already forgotten,
the day long gone, all he hears is
           the one-noted, unchanging roar
of water that is not water,
Colorado in an otherworldly key
           rising up inside him.

Listening to Shostakovich

And then the heckling bassoons,
          the violins skittering
over the flutes. The first time I heard
          that sound I believed
the urgency, the panic of the chase
          was merely a figure
of inarticulate speech. The French horn
          shrugged, the clarinets
tried smiling, and whatever "tragedy"
          rose from the cadenza,
notes on a page, was stillborn
          in midflight.

Years later I heard the concerto again.
          A snowy night, the radio's
faithful glowing. In the strings' syncopated
          gallop, there was a pressure
from the other side: a tremolo of remorse
          life disjointed by access
to cold-blooded power, how this time
          out of the hive it swarmed
to snuff me out. Then Slava struck back,
          the orchestra pursued,
and in the pinched, almost hysterical
          vibrato of the cello
I could hear my own darkness finally
          unraveling.

I turned up the fourth movement.
          The cello sung a siege
of dogged resistance, and I felt an imminence
          slide in,
a blessing, the radio's electric humming,

though the day before,
if you had asked me, I would have said
I heard nothing, and others,
friends, still tell me it doesn't exist,
the sound of voices
cracking under pressure, wind compressed
through metal apertures

in a recording studio—a figment.
The outcast angel of art
pressed its lips to my ear. March 5, 1953,
Stalin was dead.
Snow ticked on Moscow streets like
a bloodless metronome.
But here in the rising swell of the orchestra:
Kick in my door in the middle
of the night, the cello says, *I'll never be yours*
for the blacking.

Anatomy Lab

The body bags reeking of formaldehyde rested on
steel tables like butterfly cocoons
      tucked in a hatchery.
I unzipped number nineteen where you,
      or rather, the pale yellow,
darkening constellation of you, lay waiting.

It was the end of the semester. The students had sawed
through your sternum. Your lungs, burned black
from years of cigarette smoke, leaned
against your left arm. Your hand
      (the wrinkled fingers,
nails still pink with polish) twitched when
I pulled the long palmar muscle.

Give it a try, I said a little more bluntly than I expected.
      You were kind enough to overlook
my embarrassment, my awkward belief
that someone, a husband or hospice worker,
in the ice-crusted, bare blown season
      of final amends must have loved you.

Whoever you were, whatever travail of life
you called your own, even in death
      you were quicker than I was.
I pushed the split halves of your face together
      as if in the cracked chrysalis of flesh,
gone, long gone, I could still find you,
      the lucent beam,
the unmade aperture still shining
in the dust before you were born.

Heaven

1.
I moved and it moved too, matching my every
heel-turn and shimmy. At first, a scheduled shadow

and through-line I had counted on, the two of us
a pantomime of doubles, as in the mirror sequence

of Groucho and Harpo Marx in *Duck Soup* in 1930.
But then I grew up. Or maybe I shooed myself

into that dismantling stillness between
the words where thinking hadn't knocked,

where the wind waited in the honey locust tree
after everything had happened.

Not a definitive, planetary beam of insight,
not a scrubbed package or reckoning of maps,

the patio was erased. The simmering aspens
turned the volume down low so I could hear,

in the somnambulant gleaming of the neighborhood,
the grazing chur of a lawn mower, a staple gun

ka-chunking roof shingles, and despite it all,
rich with the antioxidants of listening,

ascending through layers of early morning light,
the radiant, empty, open *I am*.

2.
At least it felt that way. The undulating curtains
of fog, the deep, Romantic pockets of vision

surrendered themselves, and in their place
an awareness without views, perception

beyond a mere collecting of souvenir nametags.
I pulled out my to-do list with its tiny

corporate logo stenciled in the header:
buy soymilk and double A batteries, it said.

It no longer mattered that I was happy.
A teasing enchantment of words, the place touted

on the website had a secluded beach and free,
unlimited mini-bar access, whereas this—

an incremental unfolding, a rappelling by degrees
out of the crosshairs of another tedious habit—

sprung me with something resembling wakefulness.
I could say I was awake, and yet I didn't hold on.

The day non-derivative, thrivingly absorbent
and useless like the scent of my neighbor's

pine tree in high summer. At last, no other
purpose—no other world I had to get to.

In the Age of Loud and Louder

You could still hear it in the poker game
that broke out over a bottle
of homemade rosé at a raucous dinner party.

You could watch it crawl
in a politician's face at a press conference,
one and then another second

of unscripted bewilderment,
a stony hush, for the camera, submerged with,
integral to fomenting the bombastic

claim blurted out next.
Talking, the poet Hafiz once said,
a crazed defense of a crumbling fort.

Whereas this, which goes without saying,
a refuge, a restorative balm
that excludes no one, for some, an exile

cancelled by the luminous confabulation
of cocktail chatter. Pull up a chair,
take a load off. The revolution

will not be spoken. Here, now,
a manifesto of the unsaid,
a little silence to show you the way home.

The Great Troublemaker Says Thank You

I trusted the broken propeller, the receding
gum line and empty mailbox,
the failed story, carrier of voices,
that I possessed many such fatal velocities,
that a scorched earth policy of history
lodged inside me,
and I burned.

I trusted the sacred contract of burning.
Thrashed, pinned down
like the dirty rain turned to snow.
And then sleep, that I trusted the deeper,
more affirming loss. It opened
like a jugular, an opportunity,
that dreaming, when that is all I could do,
carried in it, inchoate
and without form,
a beginning.

I trusted the stain of beginning.
Rusty but forgiven, crusty and unleavened,
I felt the barricades unlock.
The seedpods along the runway were de-iced.
Friends, family, and career:
long odds at the roulette table.
Feelings, perceptions, and impulses:
mere decorative apparel.
I trusted I could wear them anyway.
I stood facing the day mountain,
the night houses, and they opened.

I remembered the great matter
inside me, outside me
rising like a blistered star.
You, my teacher—*What is it?* you asked.
I kicked the water bottle over.
I hurled my sharpened pencil in the flames.

Close the Book

Let the reading carry on in a different house,
in a comfy chair beneath somebody else's lamp.
Let that person hear the words in their
amniotic sloshing, in their playful pantomime
of the sea at night. Enough has been said
that maybe somewhere else will be said again
by a more outspoken, temperamental author.
Should you read that book? Will those
brassy, effervescent lines shine for you?
Will those memorable metaphors
in another tone capture the boons and banes
of the day? Close the book. Prop it back on
the shelf. Or hold it in your hands.
Feel the dust jacket as it slides along
the woven hinges. No more words. Time
for your life again—your life, as if that, too,
you had cradled on your chest beneath some
prophylactic circle of light. Turn it off.
You've been on an exquisite journey,
and for this you are grateful. But now let
the window glow as if in the opening notes
of a sublime but earthly aria in which you are
the singer, the jilted chanteuse or love-struck
troubadour ready for the next scene.
Close the book. The spell is broken.
A bowl of Cheerios and cold milk calls.
A clean spoon waits for you in the drawer.

Notes

Page 47, "Poetry Will Never Save the World": the lines in italics are from Tomaz Šalamun's poem "Drums."

Page 49, "Love Triangle": With thanks to Jorge Luis Borges.

About the Rocky Mountain Poetry Series

"To have great poets there must be great audiences, too."
—Walt Whitman

The Rocky Mountain Poetry Series publishes classic and contemporary poets of the American west, featuring both established and emerging writers. We bring out several volumes each year that we believe embody some aspect of the vitality of our region: the landscape, the history, the people and the imaginative power and diversity that articulate them and render them both recognizable and new.

The series offers no contests, competitions, prizes or awards, because those approaches divide readers by turning them into competitors. Our goal, instead, is to bring readers together, creating the greatest possible audience.

In the end, vibrant arts communities emerge only when three crucial conditions exist: enough peace to allow people to think about art, enough quiet to give them the time to learn how to make it and enjoy it, and enough of those people to come together and support it in whatever ways they can. Assuming you are not running for your life, that you have enough to eat, and that you care about poetry, we hope you will join us as a member of the community that is The Rocky Mountain Poetry Series.

—David J. Rothman, RMPS Editor

For more information about the series, please visit conundrum-press.com

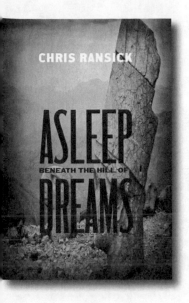

ASLEEP BENEATH THE HILL OF DREAMS

Poetry by Chris Ransick

978-1-938633-49-2
$12.99

Chris Ransick, appointed Denver Poet Laureate in 2006, is the author of five books: *Language for the Living and the Dead; Never Summer, Poems from Thin Air* (Winner of the Colorado Book Award); *A Return to Emptiness* (Colorado Book Award finalist); *Lost Songs & Last Chances*; and *Asleep Beneath the Hill of Dreams.*

MORE GREAT BOOKS FROM CONUNDRUM PRESS

ACTIVE GODS

Poetry by Michael J. Henry

978-1-938633-44-7
$12.99

"I love the atmosphere of Henry's poems, the feeling of them tilting on the edge of something. On one side: a plainspoken everyman. On the other side: a man of complex feelings and thoughts, a man who notices things about the world and its inhabitants that both delight us and break our hearts. This is what good poets do: take us to places we recognize, but through a different lens or through a new door."

—Thomas Lux, author of *Child Made of Sand*